Motivational Journal For Women

# UNLEASHING YOUR TRUE DESIRES

All You Need To Light That
Fire Within You

Tamara McBride

# Table of Contents

Chapter 1: Why You Are Amazing ............ 6
Chapter 2: Trust The Process ............ 9
Chapter 3: Top Life regrets of Dying Hospital Patients ............ 11
Chapter 4: Why Are You Working So Hard ............ 14
Chapter 5: Take Ownership of Yourself ............ 18
Chapter 6: *How to stop procrastinating.* ............ 20
Chapter 7: Meditation The Key To Happiness ............ 24
Chapter 8: Setting Too High Expectations ............ 27
Chapter 9: *Be Motivated by Challenge* ............ 31
Chapter 10: Your Work is Good Enough ............ 34
Chapter 11: Knowing When It's Time To Switch Off ............ 37
Chapter 12: *Going Through Tough Times Is Part of The Journey* ............ 40
Chapter 13: Get in the Water (Stop wasting time) ............ 43
Chapter 14: Be Inspired to Create ............ 45
Chapter 15: *Avoid The Dreaded Burnout* ............ 47
Chapter 16: Everything is A Marathon Not A Sprint ............ 50
Chapter 17: When It's Okay to Do Nothing ............ 54
Chapter 18: The Easiest Way to Live a Short, Unimportant Life ............ 58
Chapter 19: Live A Long, Important Life ............ 60
Chapter 20: How Distraction Robs You of Joy ............ 63
Chapter 21: Become A High Performer ............ 67
Chapter 22: Dealing With Inertia (Gym) Motivation ............ 71
Chapter 23: The Power of Contentment ............ 74
Chapter 24: Why Are You Working So Hard ............ 77
Chapter 25: You Will Never Regret Good Work Once It is Done ............ 81
Chapter 26: The Power of Community ............ 84
Chapter 27: Put Yourself In Positions of Opportunity ............ 87
Chapter 28: *Reach Peak Motivation* ............ 90

Chapter 29: NOTHING IS IMPOSSIBLE ............................................... 93  
Chapter 30: How To Stop Feeling Overwhelmed .................................. 96  
Chapter 31: How To Rid Yourself of Distraction ................................... 98  
Chapter 32: How To Live In The Moment (Part 2) ............................ 102  
Chapter 33: Figuring Out Your Dreams ................................................ 105  
Chapter 34: *Don't Be Demotivated By Fear* ...................................... 108  
Chapter 35: Develop A Habit of Studying............................................ 111  
Chapter 36: 9 Ways To Know If You Are A Highly Sensitive Person ................................................................................................................ 114  
Chapter 37: 7 Ways To Know When It's Time To Say Goodbye To The Past .......................................................................................... 118

# Chapter 1:
# Why You Are Amazing

When was the last time you told yourself that you were amazing? Was it last week, last month, last year, or maybe not even once in your life?

As humans, we always seek to gain validation from our peers. We wait to see if something that we did recently warranted praise or commendation. Either from our colleagues, our bosses, our friends, or even our families. And when we don't receive those words that we expect them to, we think that we are unworthy, or that our work just wasn't good enough. That we are lousy and under serving of praise.

With social media and the power of the internet, these feelings have been amplified. For those of us that look at the likes on our Instagram posts or stories, or the number of followers on Tiktok, Facebook, or Snapchat, we allow ourselves to be subjected to the validation of external forces in order to qualify our self-worth. Whether these are strangers who don't know you at all, or whoever they might be, their approval seems to matter the most to us rather than the approval we can choose to give ourselves.

We believe that we always have to up our game in order to seek happiness. Everytime we don't get the likes, we let it affect our mood for the rest of the day or even the week.

Have you ever thought of how wonderful it is if you are your best cheerleader in life? If the only validation you needed to seek was from yourself? That you were proud of the work you put out there, even if the world disagrees, because you know that you have put your heart and soul into the project and that there was nothing else you could have done better in that moment when you were producing that thing?

I am here to tell you that you are amazing because only you have the power to choose to love yourself unconditionally. You have the power to tell yourself that you are amazing. and that you have the power to look into yourself and be proud of how far you came in life. To be amazed by the things that you have done up until this point, things that other people might not have seen, acknowledged, or given credit to you for. But you can give that credit to yourself. To pat yourself on the back and say "I did a great job".

I believe that we all have this ability to look inwards. That we don't need external forces to tell us we are amazing because deep down, we already know we are.

If nobody else in the world loves you, know that I do. I love your courage, your bravery, your resilience, your heart, your soul, your commitment, and your dedication to live out your best life on this earth. Tell yourself each and everyday that you deserve to be loved, and that you are loved.

Go through life fiercely knowing that you don't need to seek happiness, validations, and approval from others. That you have it inside you all along and that is all you need to keep going.

# Chapter 2:
# Trust The Process

Today we're going to talk about the power of having faith that things will work out for you even though you can't see the end in sight just yet. And why you need to simply trust in the process in all the things that you do.

Fear is something that we all have. We fear that if we quit our jobs to pursue our passions, that we may not be able to feed ourselves if our dreams do not work out. We fear that if we embark on a new business venture, that it might fail and we would have incurred financial and professional setbacks.

All this is borne out of the fear of the unknown. The truth is that we really do not know what can or will happen. We may try to imagine in our heads as much as we can, but we can never really know until we try and experienced it for ourselves.

The only way to overcome the fear of the unknown is to take small steps, one day at a time. We will, to the best of our ability, execute the plan that we have set for ourselves. And the rest we leave it up to the confidence that our actions will lead to results.

If problems arise, we deal with it there and then. We put out fires, we implement updated strategies, and we keep going. We keep going until we have exhausted all avenues. Until there is no more roads for us to travel, no more paths for us to create. That is the best thing that we can do.

If we constantly focus on the fear, we will never go anywhere. If we constantly worry about the future, we will never be happy with the present. If we dwell on our past failures, we will be a victim of our own shortcomings. We will not grow, we will not learn, we will not get better.

I challenge each and every one of you today to make the best out of every situation that you will face. Grab fear by the horns and toss them aside as if it were nothing. I believe in you and all that you can achieve.

# Chapter 3:
# Top Life regrets of Dying Hospital Patients

The most common regret of dying people is
***"I wish I'd had the courage to live a life true to myself, not the life others expected of me."***

Why is this such a common dying regret at the end of our lives? And how can you make sure that you don't end up feeling the same way?

**How to Be Courageous and Avoid the Biggest Regret**

If you're reading this, then you probably have the power to make decisions in your daily life. Rarely, we are forced to live in a way that we don't want to live (thankfully). But somehow, many of us still end up wishing we had lived in a more true way to ourselves.

Here's why I believe this happens:

Anytime I find myself feeling stuck in neutral, it's usually the result of not having a clear target. I find myself doing work without defining what the work should be or hoping for a change without determining the underlying actions that would lead to it. In other words, I'm not clear about what I care about and how I can get there—more on this in a moment.

Here's the result:

If you never draw a line in the sand and clarify what is important to you, then you'll end up doing what's expected of you. When you don't have a clear purpose driving you forward, you default to doing what others approve of. We're not sure what we want, and so we do what we think other people want.

The gray areas in life usually arise when we haven't decided what we believe.

This is the position I think we all find ourselves in from time to time. And it's one reason why I think many of us end up living the life others expect us to live instead of a life that is true to ourselves.

I often think about how I can get better at living with purpose and live an important life instead of an urgent one. When it comes to being clear about what I'm doing and why I'm doing it, I like to use a technique that I call the Bullseye Method.

## The Bullseye Method

*"A skillful archer ought first to know the mark he aims at and then apply his hand, his bow, his string, his arrow, and his motion accordingly. Our counsels go astray because they are not rightly addressed and have no fixed end. No wind works for the man that has no intended post to sail towards."*

— Michel de Montaigne

The quote above essentially says: "If you didn't know where the target was located, you would never fire an arrow and expect to hit the bullseye."

And yet, we often live our lives this way. We wake up and face the world day after day (we keep firing arrows), but we focus on everything *except* the bullseye.

For example, if you want to get in shape, then the bullseye is to become the type of person who never misses a workout. That's on target. And yet, many of us spend our time looking for a stronger bow (workout program) or a better arrow (diet plan), or a tighter string (running shoes). Those things matter, but none of them serve you if you're not firing arrows in the right direction.

The Bullseye Method ignores the things we typically focus on, like tactics, resources, or tools. Instead, it focuses on the identity and location of the bullseye. It forces us to be clear about what we want from life.

In other words, forget about how you want to perform or what you want to look like. A bullseye is not "gain 10 pounds of muscle" or "build a successful business." The bullseye is living a life that's on target. It's having a purpose and a clear direction for the actions you will take.

What type of person do you want to become? What type of values do you want to stand for? Which actions do you want to become your habits?

The only way to live a life that is true to you is to have a purpose of organizing your life around. Where is your bullseye located?

# Chapter 4:
# Why Are You Working So Hard

Your why,

your reason to get up in the morning,

the reason you act,

really is everything - for without it, there could be nothing.

Your why is the partner of your what,

that is what you want to achieve, your ultimate goal.

Your why will be what pushes you through the hard times on the path to your dreams.

It may be your children or a burning desire to help those less fortunate,

whatever the reason may be,

it is important to keep that in mind when faced with troubles or distractions.

Knowing what you want to do, and why you are doing it,

is of imperative importance for your life.

The tragedy is that most people are aiming for nothing.

They couldn't tell you why they are working in a certain field even if they tried.

Apart from the obvious financial payment,

They have no clue why they are there.

Is financial survival alone really a good motive to act?
Or would financial prosperity be guaranteed if you pursued greater personal preference?
Whatever your ambitions or preference in life,
make sure your why is important enough to you to guarantee your persistence.

Sometimes when pursuing a burning desire,
we can become distracted from the reason we are working.

Your why should be reflected in everything you do.
Once you convince yourself that your reason is important enough, you will not stop.
Despite the hardships, despite the fear, despite the loss and pain.
As long as you maintain a steady path of faith and resilience,
your work will soon start to pay off.
A light will protrude from the darkness and the illusionary troubles sent to test your faith will disappear as if they were never here.

Your why must be strong.
Your what must be as clear as the day is to you now.
And your faith must be eternal and unwavering.
Only then will the doors be opened to you.
This dream can be real, and will be.

When it is clear in the mind with faith, the world will move to show you the way.

The way will be revealed piece by piece, requiring you to take action and do the required work to bring your dream into reality.

Your why is so incredibly important.
The bigger your why, the greater the urgency, and the quicker your action will be.

Take the leap of faith.
Do what you didn't even know you could.
Never mind anyone else.
Taking the unknown path.
Perhaps against the advice of your family and friend,
But you know what your heart wants.

You know that even though the path will be dangerous, the reward will be tremendous.
The risks of not never finding out is too great.
The risk of never knowing if you could have done better is unfathomable.
You can always do better, and you must.

Knowing what is best for you may prove to be the most important thing for you.
How you feel about the work you are doing,
How you feel about the life you are living,
And how do you make the most of the time you have on this earth.
These may prove far more important than financial reward could ever do for you.

Aim to strike a balance.

A balance between working on what you are passionate about and building a wealthy financial life.

If your why and will are strong enough,

Success is all but guaranteed for you – no second guesses needed.

Aim for the sky,

However high you make it,

you will have proven you can indeed fly.

# Chapter 5:
# <u>Take Ownership of Yourself</u>

What belongs to you but is used by other people more than you?

Your name.

And that's okay. People can use your name. But you must never allow yourself to lose ownership of you. In fact, you need to be incredibly conscious of taking ownership of everything that you are. And I do mean everything. Those few extra pounds, the nose you think is too big, your ginger hair or freckled skin. Whatever it is that you are insecure about, it's time that you showed up and took ownership. Because the moment you do your world will change.

But what does that look like? Why does it matter?

If someone parks a limo in the road outside your house, hands you the keys and tells you it is yours, what would you do? You're not just gonna put the keys in the ignition and leave it in the road. You are going to put that thing in a garage and get it insured. You will make sure that it is in a place where it is safe from weather and your jealous neighbour. Those are the things that you do when you take ownership of something. You make sure that they are protected because you value them. Then when you drive around town you don't look around as if you've stolen the thing. You drive with style and confidence. You are bold and comfortable because it belongs to you. *That* is what ownership looks like.

Now I know what you're thinking. That's easy to do with a limo, but I what I have is the equivalent of a car built before world war two. But the beautiful thing about ownership is that it does not depend on the object. It is not the thing being owned that you have to worry about, all you have to do is claim it. You've seen teenagers when they get their first car. Even if it is an old rust-bucket they drive around beaming with pride. Why? Because they know that what they have is theirs. It belongs to them and so they take ownership of it.

You have to do the same. You must take ownership of every part of you because in doing so you will keep it secure. You no longer have to be insecure about your weight if you know that that is where you are at right now. That doesn't mean you don't work for change though. It doesn't give you an excuse for stagnancy. You take accountability for your change and growth as much as you do for your present state. But in taking ownership you work towards polishing your pride, not getting rid of your low self-esteem. The difference may sound semantic, but the implications are enormous. The one allows you to work towards something and get somewhere good. The other makes it feel like you are just running away from something. And when you are running away then the only direction that matters is away – even if that means you run in circles.

Make a change today. Own yourself once more and be amazed at the rush that comes with it. With ownership comes confidence.

# Chapter 6:
## *How to stop procrastinating*:

Procrastination; perhaps the most used word of our generation. Procrastination can range from a minor issue that hurts your productivity or a significant issue that's preventing you from achieving your goals. You feel powerless, and you feel hopeless; you feel de-motivated, De-strategized, even guilty and ashamed, but all in vain.

Let me in all of you on a secret of life, the need to avoid pain and the desire to gain pleasure. That is what we consider the two driving forces of life. Repeat this mantra till it gets in the back of your head. And if you don't take control over these two forces, they'll take control over you and your entire life. The need to avoid pain is what gets us into procrastinating. We aren't willing to step out of our comfort zone, be uncomfortable, fear the pain of spending our energies, fear failure, embarrassment, and rejection. We don't simply procrastinate because there's no other choice; we procrastinate because whatever it is, we don't consider it essential to us. It's not that something meaningful for us or urgent to us, and when something doesn't feel binding to us, we tend to put it off. We link to link a lot of pain to not taking action. But what if we reversed the roles? What if we start to connect not taking action to be more painful than taking action. We have to change our perspective. See that the long-term losses of not taking action are 1000x more painful than the short-term losses of taking those actions.

Stop focusing on the short-term pain of spending your time, energy, and emotions on the tasks at hand. START focusing on the long-term pain that comes when you'll realize you're not even close to the goals you were meant to achieve.

Stop your desire to gain pleasure from the unnecessary and unimportant stuff. You would rather skip your workout to watch a movie instead. You're focusing on the pleasure, the meaningless short-term craving that'll do you no good. Imagine the pleasure we'd gain if we actually did that workout. Stop making excuses for procrastinating. Start owning up to yourself, your tasks, your goals. Set a purpose in your life and start working tirelessly towards it. Take breaks but don't lose your focus!

If you're in school and you're not getting the grades that you want, and still you're not doing anything about it, then maybe it's not a priority for you. But how do we make it meaningful? How do we make it purposeful? You need to find that motivation to get yourself going. And I promise you once you find that purpose, you'll get up early in the morning, and you'll start working to make your dreams come true.

Don't just talk about it, be about it! You were willing to graduate this year, you were willing to go to the gym and change your physique, you were willing to write that book, but what happened? You didn't make them a priority, and you eventually got tired of talking. Take a deep breath and allow yourself to make the last excuse there is that's stopping you from whatever it is that you're supposed to do. I don't have enough money; I don't write well, I don't sing well, I don't have enough knowledge, that's it. That's the last excuse you're going to make and get it over with. Aren't you tired of feeling defeated? Aren't you tired of getting beat? Aren't you tired of saying "I'll get it done soon" over and over again? To all the procrastinators, YOU. STILL. HAVE. PLENTY. OF. TIME. Don't quit, don't give up, don't just lay there doing nothing; you can make it happen. But not with that procrastinating. Set up a goal, tear it into manageable pieces, stop talking about the things you were going to do, and start doing them for real!

It's not too late for anything. There might be some signs that'll show you that you need to rest. Take them. Take the time you need to get back on track. But don't give up on the immediate gratification. Don't listen to that little voice in your head. Get out of bed, lift those weights, start working on that project, climb that mountain. You're the only person that's stopping you from achieving your goals, your dreams. With long-term success, either you're going to kick the hell out of life, or life's going to kick the hell out of you; whichever of that happens the most will become your reality. We're the master of our fates, the ambassador of our ambitions; why waste our time and lives away into doing something that won't even matter to us in a few years? Why not work towards something that will touch people, inspire them, give them hope.

I'll do it in the next hour, I'll do it the next day, I'll do it the next week, and before you know, you're dragging it to the next month or even next year. And that's the pain of life punching you in the face. The regrets of missing opportunities will eventually catch up to you. Every day you get a chance to either make the most out of life or sit on the sidelines taking the crumbles which people are leaving behind. Take what you want or settle for what's left! That's your choice.

You have to push yourself long past the point of boredom. Boredom is your worst enemy. It kills more people in the pursuit of success than anything or anyone will ever destroy. Your life just doesn't stop accidentally. It's a series of actions that you either initiate or don't initiate. Some people have already made their big decisions today, after waking up. While some, they're still dwelling on the things that don't matter. They're afraid of self-evaluation, thus wasting their time. So focus on yourself, focus on what you're doing with your time, have clarity on what you're trying to achieve. Build into what you're trying to accomplish. Between where you are and where you want to go, there's a skill set that you have to master. There's a gap that's asking for your hard work. So pay the price for what you want to become.

# Chapter 7:
# Meditation The Key To Happiness

Have you ever wondered why people who meditate tend to be the happiest, most grateful and satisfied people on earth? And have you ever wondered why the rest of us always seem to be unhappy about everything that is going on with our lives even though we are incredibly fortunate to be alive?

Many of us have a roof over our heads, smartphones that keeps us connected all the time, friends and family that surround us, but yet we still can't explain why we aren't at peace inside.

We get bogged down by traffic, people around us who seem to rub us the wrong way, and the countless other things that seem to bring us closer and closer to anguish.

Another problem that many of us have to deal with right now is stress. we have deadlines, colleagues, bosses, and paperwork that bring us overwhelm on a daily basis that we find ourselves off balance and in search of our breath.

I want to introduce you to the powerful tool called meditation, and why it is crucial that you employ it in your lives to reduce stress and anxiety and to live a more mindful life starting today.

When we meditate, even to a short 5-10min guided meditation practice that can be found on youtube or even right here on this channel, we bring our awareness to the present moment. And when we breathe and focus on the breath, we allow time for ourselves to be grounded and centered. When thoughts enter our mind, we simply acknowledge them and let them drift on by. This conscious practice of being fully present and deep breathing allows our bodies to relax and destress. And we are much more focused on what we need to do and how we can get to our goals faster.

Through meditation, one can change and rewire our brain to stop thinking of the past and future but to focus on the here and now. With intention, meditation can also help you get what you needed to done faster.

Through my own meditation practice, i have found that it made every day of my life much more purposeful and grounded. Before, i always found myself drifting throughout the day, wasting time, procrastinating, and feeling guilty for not taking action. But with a simple 10min guided meditation practice, i was able to refocus my attention and get my day going as it should without feeling sorry that i had wasted my morning not getting anything done.

Meditation takes time to develop, like a muscle, consistency is the key to success. By devoting 10mins each day to meditation, you are telling yourself that this is the time for yourself, time to reframe all the negative thoughts, to be grateful for your existence, to not dwell on the past, and to focus on the things and people that matter in life. Your body will essentially be "tricked" into automatically feeling abundance, happiness, and joy. The more you do it, the more powerful this technique becomes.

I challenge each and every one of you to try out meditation for yourself, even if i am only able to get through to one person, i am sure you will experience the rich and rewarding experience that meditation can do for you today.

# Chapter 8:
# Setting Too High Expectations

Today we're going to talk about the topic of setting too high expectations. Expectations about everything from work, to income, to colleagues, friends, partners, children, family. Hopefully by the end of this video I will be able to help you take things down a notch in some areas so that you don't always get disappointed when things don't turn out the way you expect it to.

Let's go one by one in each of these areas and hopefully we can address the points that you are actively engaged in at the moment.

Let's begin with work and career. Many of us have high expectations for how we want our work life to be. How we expect our companies and colleagues to behave and the culture that we are subjected to everyday. More often that not though, companies are in the business of profit-making and cutting costs. And our high expectations may not meet reality and we might end up getting let down. What I would recommend here is that we not set these expectations of our colleagues and bosses, but rather we should focus on how we can best navigate through this obstacle course that is put in front of us. We may want to focus instead on how we can handle ourselves and our workload. If however we find that we just can't shake off this expectations that we want from working in a company, maybe we want to look elsewhere to companies that have a work culture that suits our personality. Maybe one that is more vibrant and encourages freedom of expression.

Another area that we should address is setting high expectations of our partners and children. Remember that we are all human, and that every person is their own person. Your expectations of them may not be their expectations of themselves. When you impose such an ideal on them, it may be hard for them to live up to. Sure you should expect your partner to be there for you and for your children to behave a certain way. But beyond that everyone has their own personalities and their own thoughts and ideas. And what they want may not be in line with what we want for them. Many a times for Asian parents, we expect our kids to get good grades, get into good colleges, and maybe becoming a doctor or lawyer one day. But how many of us actually understand what our kids really want? How many of us actually listen to what our kids expect of themselves? Maybe they really want to be great at music, or a sport, or even finance. Who's to say what's actually right? We should learn to trust others and let go of some of our own expectations of them and let them become whoever they want to be.

The next area I want to talk about is simply setting too high expectations of yourself. Many times we have an ideal of who we want to be - how we want to look, how we want our bodies to look, and how we want our bank statement to look, amongst many others. The danger here is when we set unrealistic expectations as to when we expect these things to happen. Remember most things in life takes time to happen. The sooner you realise that you need more time to get there, the easier it will be on yourself. When we set unrealistic timelines, while it may seem ideal to rush through the process to get results fast, more often than not we are left disappointed when we don't hit them. We then get discouraged and may even feel like a failure or give up the whole process entirely. Wouldn't it be better if we could give ourselves more time for nature to work its magic? Assuming you follow the steps that you have laid out and the action plans you need to take, just stretch this timeline out a little farther to give yourself more breathing room. If you feel you are not progressing as fast as you had hoped, it is okay to seek help and to tweak your plans as they go along. Don't ever let your high expectations discourage you and always have faith and trust in the process even when it seems hard.

One final thing I want to talk about is how we can shift from setting too high expectations to one of setting far-out goals instead. There is a difference. Set goals that serve to motivate you and inspire you to do things rather than ones that are out of fear. When we say we expect something, we immediately set ourselves up for disappoint. However if we tell ourselves that we really want something, or that we want to achieve something that is of great importance to us, we shift to a goal-oriented mindset. One that is a lot healthier. We no longer fear the deadline creeping up on us. We instead continually work on getting there no matter how long it takes. That we tell ourselves we will get there no matter what, no matter how long. The key is to keep at it consistently and never give up.

Having the desire to work at an Apple store as a retail specialist, I never let myself say that I expect apple to hire me by a certain time otherwise I am never pursuing the job ever again. Rather I tell myself that being an Apple specialist is my dream job and that I will keep applying and trying and constantly trying to improve myself until Apple has no choice but to hire me one day. A deadline no longer bothers me anymore. While I wait for them to take me in, I will continue to pursue other areas of interest that will also move my life forward rather than letting circumstances dictate my actions. I know that I am always in control of my own ship and that I will get whatever I put my mind to eventually if I try hard enough.

So with that I challenge each and every one of you to be nicer to yourselves. Lower your lofty expectations and focus on the journey instead of the deadline. Learn to appreciate the little things around you and not let your ego get in the way.

I hope you learned something today, take care and I'll see you in the next one.

# Chapter 9:

## ***Be Motivated by Challenge***

You have an easy life and a continuous stream of income, you are lucky! You have everything you and your children need, you are lucky! You have your whole future planned ahead of you and nothing seems to go in the other direction yet, you are lucky!

But how far do you think this can go? What surety can you give yourself that all will go well from the start to the very end?

Life will always have a hurdle, a hardship, a challenge, right there when you feel most satisfied. What will you do then?

Will you give up and look for an escape? Will you seek guidance? Or will you just give up and go down a dark place because you never thought something like this could happen to you?

Life is full of endless possibilities and an endless parade of challenges that make life no walk in the park.

You are different from any other human being in at least one attribute. But your life isn't much different than most people's. You may be less fortunate or you may be the luckiest, but you must not back down when life strikes you.

This world is a cruel place and a harsh terrain. But that doesn't mean you should give up whenever you get hit in the back. That doesn't mean you don't catch what the world throws at you.

Do you know what you should do? Look around and observe for examples. Examples of people who have had the same experiences as you had and what good or bad things did they do? You will find people on both extremes.

You will find people who didn't have the courage or guts to stand up to the challenge and people who didn't have the time to give up but to keep pushing harder and harder, just to get better at what they failed the last time.

The challenges of life can never cross your limits because the limits of a human being are practically infinite. But what feels like a heavy load, is just a shadow of your inner fear dictating you to give up.

But you can't give up, right? Because you already have what you need to overcome this challenge too. You just haven't looked into your backpack of skills yet!

If you are struggling at college, go out there and prove everyone in their wrong. Try to get better grades by putting in more hours little by little.

If people take you as a non-social person, try to talk to at least one new person each day.

If you aren't getting good at a sport, get tutorials and try to replicate the professionals step by step and put in all your effort and time if you truly care for the challenge at hand.

The motivation you need is in the challenge itself. You just need to realize the true gains you want from each stone in your path and you will find treasures under every stone.

# Chapter 10:
# Your Work is Good Enough

We, humans, are genetically coded to get mad at people getting better at things than us, if not jealous.

These feelings may not bother us right now, and they might never. But these feelings are a leech on their own. They need one to feel low on their self-esteem and may never get ahead of our selves.

We get caught in a competition that no one else imposed on us but we ourselves decided to step into it.

So what we want is one thing, but what we have and we don't want is a whole new problem. We look at one thing and want it instantly without even weighing it side by side with what we already have.

What you have right now is something you have worked for till now. It is something your fate has chosen for you. This is what might be the best for you. You don't necessarily need something better that you like over what you already have. You just need to come to terms with what you have right now and perfect your craft.

You want something more because you are not content with everything you have and everything you do. It is natural to feel this way. It is normal to want more. But it is never OK to leave a thing incomplete and just because you haven't got a hold of things yet.

Things often seem wrong. We feel like an Impostor every time we come up with something new.

Everything we do seem to be a derivative of something someone else has done because we rarely come across a unique idea these days. And even when we come across one, someone else gets the same epiphany. So we never get ahead of ourselves and compete with what is on our hands.

You already have a lot in your hands to take care of so you don't need to pet more worries. You don't need to feed your brain more weaknesses of yourself than you already have.

We all need to realize a simple fact. The fact is that no matter how much we try to second guess our achievements or failures for that matter, we will always finally come to realize that we were right the first time.

You were RIGHT the FIRST TIME. So you only needed to overcome the fight within you.

The first time we do something good, we instantly know that we have something good going on. But then we try to see through others' eyes and lose our own sight of the bigger goals.

So your work is never based on your luck, but only on your talent and devotion. And if no one steps up to give you a round of applause, you still have your own will and mind to be the best judge and critic of your deed. But you also need to become the biggest mentor and coach of your own vessel. Because no vessel without a knock shows its presence.

# Chapter 11:
# Knowing When It's Time To Switch Off

Today I'm going to talk about relaxation and off-work time. I hope that by the end of this discussion that I can get you to calm down and just enjoy life a little bit more. Life isn't all about work and no play. We must learn to set boundaries and learn when it is time to work and when it is time to swift off.

For many of us who are workaholics, or those with immensely busy schedules and deadlines, we may find it hard to chill. Having all these problems in the back of our minds, our day becomes consumed with work that we may find it incredibly difficult to disconnect from. We may end up growing distant and not being present with our families when they require our attention. This can affect our relationships negatively in a multitude of ways.

For those of you who have children, not knowing when to switch off and give your full attention to their upbringing can have direct consequences to their growth and development. Furthermore, your children may view you as distant and disengaged. Not being able to get that parental support from you, they may not view you as a pillar of support. Over time your children may learn not to look for you when they need help because you are always either busy with work or too preoccupied to engage with them.

The same goes for your partner. If they don't get the full attention from you during dinner conversations, or that you are constantly replying emails on your phone and messaging your colleagues at all hours of the evening, they might also grow distant to you over time. You see relationships are built on quality time spent together. Whether it be with friends, family, partners, or kids. They all operate on the same principle. Which is why knowing when to switch off and give your relationships the quality time it needs is very important.

Not knowing when to switch off also has other consequences. It robs us of joy. It robs us of our free time because we don't set boundaries between work and play. We give our colleagues 24 hour assess to us, knowing that we will be available all hours of the day no matter the time. This frequent intrusion into our personal time is unfortunately the culture that some companies choose to adopt. Depending on how you feel about it and your circumstance, it is my opinion that this isn't the best work culture to be in if it happens all year round.

When your employers expect you to work past your work hours every single day, you might want to think twice about whether this sacrifice is worth your time and money. Whether the trade off is worth putting your relationships and obligations on the line. Whether your time is worth more or less than the company is paying to take away from you. Only you can make that decision for yourself.

Another problem that all of us face with the pandemic is that many of us are forced to work from home. While this can sound like a good thing for many of us, in some ways it can make it difficult to draw the line between work and rest. Having the freedom to work all hours of the day makes it harder for us to stay focused on the job, and many times we can't separate the parts of the day that is meant for work and the parts that are meant for rest. Studies have shown that we spend more time working when we are at home because we simply don't know when it is time to stop and switch off.

This phenomenon actually resonates with me as I too work from home. And my work day tends to stretch from the minute I wake up, to the last hour before I hit the hay. Setting clear boundaries becomes much more difficult and requires a great deal of discipline.

To sum it all up, knowing when to switch off actually requires an active commitment on our part to set the boundaries we need and to stick to it religiously. We should define the time of day in our week that are meant for work and the times that are meant for family and friends. And that means no work calls, no emails, no checking on company group messages, and no work laptops during those times.

By following these rules strictly, we can then give ourselves the time and space we need to recharge, rest, spend time with family, and then come back to work ready for another day.

# Chapter 12:

# *Going Through Tough Times Is Part of The Journey*

For someone going through tough times, for someone going through the same hardships, again and again, every day, you are trying but not getting used to all this.

Things never seem to get better and you don't think you are just right there to get a hold of things. You think you will get them this time, but they always seem to be going a new way that you never planned.

It's alright! You are not the first one to think about things this way are you certainly won't be the last one.

You are not the first person to think that you will have different achievements this time. You are not the first person to think that you will achieve bigger goals this year. You are not the first person to fail at every corner after all that determination and grit.

Life always kicks us on the blindside, and most of us know what it feels like. But not all of us want to stay in the bed all day and feel sorry for ourselves for what happened before.

People always find a way to cope with the tragedies of life. And these people know the true purpose of life. They know the true definition of life. Wanna know what that is? It's the hard times that make you a harder more precious gem.

You can never possibly understand why it is happening to you because it is what it is and you can never set your back to reality.
The reality is that no one has ever lived a reasonable life without facing the hard times. And only the people who smiled back at these hard times had a happy ending in the end.

The only thing that makes us go through life with a smile in the hope of getting a big reward at the end of it all. Our lives aren't judged on the number of success stories we write, but with the techniques, we adapt to tackle the moments when life pushes us against a wall.

It won't always be your fault but it might be your luck trying to test your limits. So why don't you show it?

Things will always go wrong in your life but that doesn't make it justifiable to put everything aside and start mourning and regretting your every mistake and every flaw. But it's time to start removing those flaws to minimize your mistakes and trying to be a perfect individual.

This is the journey to perfection that makes going through hard times justifiable. Because every stone that your pick and set aside is another hurdle being cleared for an easier road to the top.

What happens to you in life is just a glimpse of the reality, but what you do about those things in life is what living this life is actually about.

Always remember, you and your life are always like a plane. You both fly against the winds but never along it.

# Chapter 13:
# **Get in the Water (Stop wasting time)**

Stop wasting time.

If you have something to do, then do it. It is literally that simple. Nobody likes something hanging over their head, it is stressful and pressurising and the longer you leave it, the more of a challenge it is going to be. Just get it done.

It's like getting into cold water. You can start by dipping your big toe in, then walking away and reconsidering, before putting all five of them in, maybe if you are feeling frisky you'll put in your whole foot. It is such a waste. You know you are going to get in the water eventually so you might as well dive in. Otherwise, you will spend 80% of your time drawing out an adjustment that could literally take a few seconds. What is the point? Just dive in and get it over with. Does it take a bigger first-off effort, yes. But it saves you so much time and energy afterwards. After the initial shock and a few seconds of feeling like your skin is trying to shrivel up, you are fine.

If we can do it with cold water then we can do it with that email, project or book. You can dive right into all that research you need to do. Yes, it seems overwhelming, and that first leap is going to be full of questions and discomfort. Mid-air you will probably be asking what you got yourself into but the great thing is that you can't stop mid-air. There's no turning around and floating on the air until you reach solid ground again. You are committed now.

The powerful thing is that 90% percent of your problem is inertia. It is that first step. It's sitting down, firing up your laptop and starting to work. It is getting past the idea that you have so much work to do and just focussing on what you can do right now. But when it comes down it you must realise that there is no work around for that. You cannot not do that first step. Even if it is just a passion you know that passion is going to keep burning you up on the inside until you allow it to burst out. There's no getting past the cold water, there is only getting into it. So you might as well jump. If you are trying to write a book, then sit down and just start typing. Even if you are not even typing words, just sit down for 25 minutes and type away at your keyboard. Then, while you are typing you will realise that you are sitting down and pressing the keys anyways so they may as well say something that make sense. I don't care if what you type is cliché because at this point we are not worried about quality. I don't care how good your form is in your butterfly stroke if you are not even in the water. You just need to get started so that you are moving. And once you are moving you can maximise on your momentum.

# Chapter 14:
# **Be Inspired to Create**

Some of you will look in the mirror today and think that you are weird. You will see that you are different to other people. That you are quirky or odd. But I want to encourage you. Not only is your uniqueness something that you should embrace but it is perhaps your greatest asset. The wonderful thing about people being different is that they think a little differently, see the world from a slightly different perspective. The combination of the various bits of knowledge that they have fit together in different ways.

When you speak you are most likely not conscious of your accent. Maybe if you live in a foreign country you are hyper aware of it. But how many of you know that your mind has an accent too. It has an accent that is formed from your experiences. Your experiences with pain. Your experiences with joy. Your experiences with success, failure and even your experiences with the everyday mundane. Not only that but the accent of your mind constantly evolves.

Why does that matter?

Because it is that accent which enables you to innovate. When you speak a foreign word, it takes on a new form in your accent – sometimes it may even be a sound that has never been uttered with that tone and inflection. It is completely original not because of the form of the word but because of the accent that informs the way the word comes out.

The same is true of your mind. You can speak the same ideas, study the same fields, even research the exact same thing and still end up with different outcomes. How? Because your outcomes are being informed by your experiences. Your ideas are your present thoughts running rampant through familiar thought patterns. They are tailored towards a particular style. For some of you it is like your mind rolls the r's in your ideas. It adds a certain *je ne sais quoi* to your ideas. To others your accent is thick and mutes the aesthetic nuances of ideas – manifesting in wonders of logic and mechanics.

Whatever it may be, I encourage you to embrace the accent of your mind. Actually, I demand you to. It is time that you stopped denying the world of your contribution to it. It's time that you got inspired to create. It is time that you allowed ideas to implode within the realm of your consciousness and innovations to pour out of it. Whether you find your language in art, dance, engineering, or politics. If you have a niche area of knowledge or see a pattern from a unique combination of information then it is about time you harnessed that and rode the creation train to wherever it may take you. I can promise you that you will never look back. We tend to regret the things we did not do, not the things that we did.

Listen closely and hear the accentuation of your thoughts. Then speak their creative ingenuity into being.

Create something that only you can.

# Chapter 15:
# *Avoid The Dreaded Burnout*

Do you often lack the energy to get on with any new task and feel sluggish throughout most of your day? Do you feel the burden of work that keeps getting pilled up each day?

I know we all try our best to manage everything on our hands and try to bring out the best in us. But while doing so, we engage in too many things and ultimately they take their toll.

It is becoming easier and easier every day where people have more work than ever on their hands. And their sole motive throughout life becomes, to find more and better ways of earning a better living. To find more things to be good and successful at.

We all have things on our hands to complete but let me tell you one thing. You won't be able to continue much longer if you keep with this burnout and exhaustion.

Our body is an engine and it needs a way of cooling down and tuning. So what's the first step you need to reduce burnout? You need to get the right amount of sleep.

There is this myth that you sleep one-third of your life so you don't need an 8-hour sleep. You can easily do the same with four hours and use the other four for more work. Trust me, this is not a myth, it is a misconception about proven research. Your body organs deserve at least half the time of what they spend serving us.

We can refresh and better our focus and cognitive skills once we have a good night's sleep full of dreams.

Another thing that most of us avoid doing is to say No to anyone anytime. The thing is that we don't have any obligation to anyone unless we are bound by a contract of blood or law to do or say anything that anyone tells us to do. The more we feel obligated to anyone, the more we try to do to impress that person or entity with our efforts and conduct.

This attitude isn't healthy for any relation. Excess of anything has never brought any good to anyone. So don't give up everything on just one thing. Instead, try to devise a balance between things. Over-commitment is never a good idea.

The third and final thing I want you to do is to give up on certain things at certain times. You don't need to carry your phone or laptop with you all day. This only creates a distraction even when you don't need to be in that environment.

You don't need to train your subconscious to be always alert on your emails and notifications or any incoming calls all day long. But sometimes you just need to give up on these things and zone out of your repetitive daily life.

Doing your best doesn't always mean giving yourself all out. Sometimes the best productive thing you can do is to relax. And that, my friends, can help you climb every mountain without ever getting tired of trying t do the same trail.

# Chapter 16:
# Everything is A Marathon Not A Sprint

Ask your parents, what was it like to raise children till the time they were able to lift their weight and be self-sufficient. I am sure they will say, it was the most beautiful experience in their lives. But believe me, They are lying.

There is no doubt in it that what you are today is because of your parents, and your parents didn't rest on their backs while a nanny was taking care of you.

They spent countless nights of sleeplessness changing diapers and soothing you so that you can have a good night's sleep. They did that because they wanted to see a part of them grow one day and become what they couldn't be. What you are today is because of their continuous struggle over the years.

You didn't grow up overnight, and your parents didn't teach you everything overnight. It took years for them to teach you and it took even more time for you to learn.

This is life!

Life is an amalgamation of little moments and each moment is more important than the last one.

Start with a small change. Learn new skills. The world around you changes every day. Don't get stuck in your routine life. Expand your horizons. What's making you money today might not even exist tomorrow. So why stick to it for the rest of your life.

You are never too old to learn new things. The day you stop learning is the last day of your life. A human being is the most supreme being in this universe for a reason. That reason is the intellect and the ability to keep moving with their lives.

You can never be a millionaire in one night. It's a one-in-billion chance to win a lottery and do that overnight. Most people see the results of their efforts in their next generation, but the efforts do pay off.

If you want to have eternal success. It will take an eternity of effort and struggles to get there. Because life is a marathon and a marathon tests your last breaths. But when it pays off, it is the highest you can get.

Shaping up a rock doesn't take one single hit, but hundreds of precision cuts with keen observation and attention. Life is that same rock, only bigger and much more difficult.

Changing your life won't happen overnight. Changing the way you see things won't happen overnight. It will take time.

To know everything and to pretend to know everything is the wrong approach to life. It's about progress. It's about learning a little bit at each step along the way.

To evolve, to adapt, to figure out things as they come, is the process of life that every living being in this universe has gone through before and will continue to go through in the future. We are who we are because of the marathon of life.

Every one of us today has more powerful things in our possessions right now than our previous 4 generations combined. So we are lucky to be in this world, in this era.

We have unlimited resources at our disposal, but we still can't get things in the blink of an eye. Because no matter how evolved we are, we still are a slave to the reality of nature, and that reality is the time itself!

If you are taking each step to expect a treat at each stop, you might not get anything. But if you believe that each step that you take is a piece in a puzzle, a puzzle that becomes a picture that is far beautiful and meaningful, believe me, the sky is your limit.

Life is a set of goals. You push and grind to get these goals but when you get there you realize that there is so much more to go on and achieve.

Committing to a goal is difficult but watching your dreams come true is something worth fighting for.

You might not see it today, you might not see it 2 years from now, but the finish line is always one step closer. Life has always been and always will be a race to the top. But only the ones who make it to the top have gone through a series of marathons and felt the grind throughout everything.

Your best is yet to come but is on the other end of that finish line.

# Chapter 17:
# When It's Okay to Do Nothing

Today I'm going to talk about the topic of when it is okay to do nothing. We're going to be really specific with this one, and that is talking about relaxation and switching off for a while if we feel like life just seems a little too stressful or hard to take.

For many of us who are leading busy lives, life can seem like one big endless to-do list. We attract problems everyday - whether it be from our jobs, our relationships, or children, our parents, our friends, our hobbies, there just doesn't seem like a time when we can just simply do nothing. We are constantly told to keep busy with our lives, to always be doing something, to always be productive, that we forget that sometimes doing nothing may be the best thing once in a while.

As life gets more complicated, so do our problems and responsibilities. From managing a family, paying our bills, being on time with our taxes, expenses, moving houses, changing jobs, we never run out of things to fill our time with. We expand our resources with time and energy day in and day out, never resting, and it takes a huge toll on our bodies physically, mentally, emotionally, and spiritually.

When we operate on such a high level every single day, sometimes even on auto-pilot due to the routine nature of things, we might end up losing sight of who we are and why we are placed on this Earth. We may start to forget why we are doing what we are doing and we simply get lost in the ocean of tasks that need to be completed.

Many of us think that travel is the best time to recharge and relax - but for many of us who plan elaborate trips, travel can sometimes be as exhausting as going to work although with a different agenda. With the limited time we have on our travel and leaves that we are allowed to take, we jam pack our schedule that requires detailed planning and execution. Rushing from place to place to check off landmarks of interests can sometimes be a chore in itself. If we are not careful, even travel can drain us the same way. So what should we do then?

How about nothing?

How about absolutely nothing.

Doing nothing might sound curious to many of you. "What do you mean do nothing?" Some of you might say. It is exactly what it says.

When we have nothing on our agenda, nothing to plan for and nothing to deal with, we find ourselves in a space of our own. A space where we can reflect on the things that are happening in our lives. A space where we can look inwards to check on our current state and feelings. To get in touch with ourselves to see the areas where we might want to improve on. And to be reminded of the direction that we are headed.

You can do nothing by simply finding a quiet place in your house or elsewhere, where you decide to give however long you need to recharge holistically. To make "doing nothing" successful, you have to set yourself up for success. Decide that you will switch off all electronic devices - to purge yourself of technology, of reminders, of deadlines, of your bosses and colleagues, and to find your inner quiet.

If you find sitting quietly and being by yourself can be too daunting of a task, consider finding a guided meditation guide or some soothing music where you can just simply lie and rest uninterrupted. If sleep is what you need in that moment, take a nap. If ideas flash before you, acknowledge them, write them down, your call. Listen to your body and respond to it.

When you practice doing nothing consistently, you will feel that life starts to slow down a little bit more. You start to breathe a little slower and life becomes slightly more manageable when you learn how to take care of yourself.

Instead of only looking forward to holidays and trips to recharge, learn to schedule doing nothing routinely in your calender. Having the ability and power to choose as and when you need to relax and give full and total attention to yourself is as important as the attention and time you give to those around you. Only when you can take care of yourself first can you also take care of others with the same capacity.

So I challenge each and every one of you to put yourself first by making the decision to do nothing. That it is perfectly okay to switch off the crazy life around you for a moment. You can always come back to it once you're fully recharged and ready to rumble again.

I hope you learned something today. Take care and I'll see you in the next one.

# Chapter 18:
# The Easiest Way to Live a Short, Unimportant Life

An essential and successful life may seem intriguing but, sometimes it's just a lot of work. Whereas, in comparison, a short and unimportant life seems easier to live. The one reason for this may be that you need to eat up your surroundings. People who donate to this world live longer. So, you don't donate. You consume the world. But there is no doubt that people who live longer have many advantages, whereas someone living a short life would not have time for that. Not only is it a loss, but it will affect your life in which you are breathing already.

Few things can lead a person to an unimportant and unhealthy lifestyle. Of course, no one can control how many days we will live on this planet but, we can contribute to our surroundings. And even if you come up with small things, they can impact your life somehow. Be yourself when it comes to shaping. Don't let this world shape you but yourself. It may not only change your life but, it can also give them the confidence to others to change their lives.

It would help if you believed that you could live. If you give up on your life, life will give up on you. Keep yourself worth running in every factor of life. It would be best if you made yourself feel worth it to keep up with the world. Live a meaningful life by all means. How? By contributing to things, talk with a friend, take a long walk in the mornings, or call the people you care about. Even saying hi to a stranger count as contributing to this world. And small contribution leads towards a more significant source of the outcome.

Talk with yourself about how you are going to live this life, and live, not survive. Thet both are different things. We won't know if tomorrow will be our last day, so we got to live it today as it is. Nowadays, we tend to live our lives by ourselves. We prefer to talk on the phone instead of meeting up. It just leads towards an unhealthy and unimportant life. Meet up if you can. Contribute your ideas or decisions to that plan. Make sure that you work out your best if you want it to be done.

A short and unimportant life may seem easier to live by but, it's non-enjoyable. It's full of disadvantages and losses from every side. Isn't it better to live? To give it all your best? We need to devote most of ourselves to this one life that we got. And live each day to its fullest.

# Chapter 19:
# Live A Long, Important Life

Do you think you are more capable to deal with the failure or the regret of not trying at all?

Are you living the life you want or the life everyone else wants for you?

Would you feel good spending your time on entertainment that might not last for long? Or would you feel good feeling like you are growing and have a better self of you to look at in the mirror?

Similarly, would like to live in the present or would you love to work for a better future?

Do you want money to dictate your life or do you want money to follow you where ever you go?

Would you prefer being tired or being broke?

Do you want to spend the rest of your life in this place where you and your parents were born? Or do you won't go around the world and find new possibilities in even the most remote places?

Would you rather risk it all or play it safe?

We are often presented with all these questions in our lifetime. Most people take these questions as a way to enter into your adulthood. The answers to these questions are meant to show you the actual meaning of life.

So what is Life? Life is not your parents, your work, your friends, your events, and your functions. It's within you and around you.

You should learn to live your life to the fullest. You should love to live your life for as long as you can with a happy body and a healthy mind.

A happy and healthy body and mind are important. Because you can only feel secure on a stable platform. You can only wish to stand on a platform where you know you can stay put for a long time.

There is nothing wrong with working eight or nine hours in your daily life. It's not unhealthy or anything. Working is what gives our life a purpose. Working is what keeps us active, moving, and motivated.

We have one life, and we have to make it matter. But the way we chose to do it is what matters the most. Our choices make us who we are rather than our actions.

The life we live is the epitome of our intentions and morals. We can be defined in a single word or a single phrase if we ever try. We don't need to analyze someone else, we just need to see ourselves in the mirror and we might be able to see right across the image.

The day we are able to do that, might be the day we have actually made a worthy human being of ourselves and have fulfilled our destiny.

If you are able to look at yourself and go through your whole life in the blink of an eye and cherish the memories as if you were right there at that moment. Believe me, you have had a long and important life to make you think of it all over again every day.

# Chapter 20:
# How Distraction Robs You of Joy

How many of you crave the satisfaction that distraction brings you? Whether it be checking your phone regularly for messages, or scrolling through social media apps such as Facebook, instagram, or even mindlessly browsing through streaming apps such as youtube or netflix in search of some form of content that can take your attention away from the work that is actually in front of you that you should be working on?

I believe that many of us crave these distractions because of a few key reasons. Let us see if any of these sound familiar to you, and after I've identified them i will tell you why distraction is actually not the answer to your problems.

The first reason is that we are probably bored and we want to fill that boredom with stuff just so that we can keep ourselves busy and to pass time. I would raise my hand and say that I am guilty of that.

The second reason is that we are probably subconsciously unhappy with what we are doing, whether it be our jobs, or our careers, we feel that we are not doing what we are meant to do and it is causing us anxiety, fear, and worry, and we turn to distractions as a form of therapy to try and calm our nerves, or just temporarily forget our problems for just enough time to feel good before we begin our work again. Does that sound like you?

The third reason is that we are just so engrossed in the new world of information consumption that we have become so addicted to our smartphones or smart appliances, that we willingly give 1/3 of our day away to be mindlessly consuming content that is not beneficial to our lives on this earth. The abundance of apps, streaming platforms, and mobile games, have given us a portal into another dimension away from the physical world. This distracts us from the important stuff we need to do every day to better our lives such as building meaningful relationships with friends, spending time with loved ones, and being present in whatever you are doing.

So why is distraction so harmful that it robs us of real joy and happiness?

From a physiological standpoint, distraction actually uses up a lot of our cognitive capacity to switch from a tasks which requires deep focus. When you are very productive, your brain is actually in a flow state of mind where productivity becomes much easier to achieve. You have undivided attention to complete the task at hand and your brain is working to the best of its ability to provide you with the information that you need to solve whatever problems the job requires. But when you receive a text or decide to take a quick break to check your phone and to scroll through social media, you are actually snapped out of that flow state of mind. And your mind goes into a passive state. And as you revert back to the task you were originally doing, not even mentioning the inertia and the amount of energy it takes to restart your work, your brain actually has to go through the painful process of connecting those cells from your working memory once again. costing you immense amounts of resources and energy. And as you do this probably tens of times each hour, you lose more and more of that focus and eventually you feel tired and unproductive.

And as you spiral downwards, your level of satisfaction drops and so does your sense of joy because you feel unaccomplished, you've wasted hours of time, and you may even start beating yourself up for such a poor performance.

So what action steps can you do to free yourself from distraction so that you can regain control of your energy and time?

Well the very first step, which is probably the simplest but harder to do, is to put your phone on silent mode, or keep it somewhere out of sight so that you are not tempted to reach for it. Turn off all possible forms of distraction that can jeopardise your workflow. And refrain from taking breaks as much as you can, even going to the toilet. Every minute you step away from what you are doing will cost you some form of energy in one way or another. You can even download the app "forest" which actually locks your phone down for a duration you have set for yourself, while at the same time planting a beautiful tree in your garden. It is quite rewarding to see that you have grown a tree after spending a full hour working. And as you feel more productive, your level of happiness will increase from the sense of accomplishment you feel that you got your work done in record time.

The next thing you can do is to start re-assessing the work you are doing. Ask yourself if you are truly happy at your job, because maybe u use distraction as an escape which could indicate that you are probably not doing what you were meant to do. If you really loved your job, you will be in a state of mind where your job doesn't even feel like job anymore and you just want to keep working because you are passionate about it. If that means changing your careers or trying something new, don't be afraid to do so.

The final step is to constantly remind yourself of the value of time and that time is not infinite. We only have so many hours in a day, do we really want to spend half of it on things on mindless content that does not improve ourselves as a person? Time is precious and we should spend it as wisely as we can, free of distraction, and doing meaningful work to better someone else's lives. And as we do these things, we can slowly start to regain control, which helps us become more self-disciplined. And this loop reinforces the good principles we should follow to achieve success and happiness.

# Chapter 21:
# Become A High Performer

We were put on this planet because we were meant to be all we could become. Human beings are the sum of their acts and achievements. But not everyone is capable of doing things to their full potential.

Every man's biggest burden is his or her unfulfilled potential.

So what you need to become a high-performing individual in this modern era of competition is to idolize the best of the best.

You will need to understand the real-life features of a successful individual and what you need to do to become one.

If you want to be more successful in your life you need to become obsessive. Start your day with a goal and try your best to achieve it before you head to bed. You don't necessarily need to be on the right path with the first step, but you will find the best route once you have the undefeated will to find that path.

If you want to be more developed in your life you need to sleep effectively. The most successful people have a mantra of high performing routine. They don't sleep more than five hours a day and work seven days a week. They only take one day a week to sleep more just to rejuvenate their brains and body.

If you want to know if you are a high-performing successful person, look into your body language. If you find ease and leisure in everyday tasks, You are surely not standing up to your potential. If you like to sit for a conversation, start to stand. If you like to walk, start running. Get out of your comfort zone and start thinking and acting differently.

The last thing before you start your search for the right path to excellence is to set a goal every day. Increase your creativity by finding new ways to shorten the time of you becoming the better you and finally getting what you deserve.

You will eventually start seeing your life get on the track of productive learning and execution.

Change your way of treating others, especially those who are below you. If you are not a jolly person when you are broke, you can never be a jolly person when you are rich.

Never underestimate someone who is below you. You never know to whom the inspiration might take you. You have to consider the fact that life is ever-changing. Nothing ever stays the same. People never stay where they are for long.

It is the alternating nature of life that makes you keep fighting and pushing harder for better days. That is why you work hard on your skills to become a hearty human with the arms of steel.

Most people live a quiet life of desperation where they have a lot to give and a lot to say but can never get out of their cocoons.

But you are not every other person. You are the most unique soul god has created to excel at something no one has ever thought or seen before.

Start loving yourself. Stop finding faults in yourself. You are the best version of yourself, you just haven't found the right picture to look into it yet.

You want to be a high performer in every aspect of your life, here is my final advice for you.

If you push your limits in even the smallest tasks of your life, if you stretch your mind and imagination, if you can push the rules to your benefit, you might be the happiest and the most successful man humankind has ever seen.

Keep working for your dreams till the day you die. Life opens its doors to the people who knock on it. The purpose of this life is to knock on every door of opportunity and grasp that opportunity before anyone else steps forward.

You won't fulfill your desires till you make the desired effort, and that comes with a strong will and character. So keep doing what you want to never have a regret.

# Chapter 22:
# Dealing With Inertia (Gym) Motivation

Inertia, oh dear inertia, if only there was something i can do to make you go away.

Today we are going to talk about why Inertia is so deterimental to anyone's success and how a lack of motivation can prevent you from taking that step forward to your goals.
If you don't know already, inertia is a powerful force that pulls you back from doing something that would move the needle in your life, it is like a magnet attracting you and telling you to stay and slack a little more, to lie in bed just a little longer, to keep scrolling Instagram for one more hour because it wouldn't make a difference, or to watch another episode of Netflix while the task just sits on the desk far away from your existence,

Why do I know about inertia so well? Because i struggle with it on a near hourly basis. Inertia knows me so well that it knows exactly what it needs to do or say to keep my staying for one more minute which could turn into hours and before i know it the day is over.

I deal with inertia while trying to get out of bed, get out of the house, and even going to the gym. All these are small but significant personal struggles that rob me of precious time everyday. Inertia battles with my will power on a constant basis that many times it is frankly very difficult to win.

So what can one do to beat inertia to do the things that needs to be done? Sheer determination to win by giving yourself no choice but to get started. You see, inertia can only hold you back for so long, but once you have backed yourself into a corner, you are left with no option but to start. This could mean deleting your Netflix app for just one moment, and turning off wifi, or telling yourself no lunch until you get your ass to the gym. This trick has worked on me time and time again. You see the goal is not to never watch Netflix again, but the act of getting started on your work. For me, once I have tricked my brain into turning the first page, it becomes a lot easier to keep doing the work because my brain doesn't have to keep switching from a mode of relaxation to a mode of working.

You will realise that inertia is like a rubber band, it pulls and pulls but once it snaps, it can't hold u back any longer. And you are free to pursue your day as you see fit. Inertia usually lingers the strongest in the earlier part of the day especially after you have just woken up from bed, but it can also creep up on you at anytime once you have let your guard down and prevented your creative juices from flowing from your powerful brain.

For many of us who have a 9-5 job, inertia is not so much of a problem as you are forced to get up at a specific time of day and to get to office and sit on your desk. And by the time you are at the office 1-2 hours after you have gotten out of bed, the rustiness and inertia would most likely have faded as you are left with no choice but to start your day of work.

Inertia is a 100x greater challenge for those who are entrepreneurs, freelance workers, or those who work from home. Because the freedom to choose your own work schedule means you are not being constantly overlooked by your boss to see if you are actually doing work, and leaving self discipline to yourself can be a dangerous thing with no one to supervise.

With freedom comes responsibility, and without self discipline, one can fall into the trap of easily telling oneself that it is perfectly okay to slack just one more minute. And this can turn into a habit that becomes hard to quit. Inertia is born from habit. And as you know, to break a bad habit one has to also simultaneously form a new healthier and stronger habit that can overpower the other.

So I challenge each and everyone of you to start forming a healthy habit of not procrastinating, of not letting inertia win, and over time, it will have a less and less hold on you anymore until one day you can simply shake it off and start beginning your quest of the day to get you one step closer to your goals.

# Chapter 23:
# The Power of Contentment

Today we're going to talk about why contentment is possibly a much more attainable and sustainable alternative than trying to achieve happiness.

As we have briefly gone through in the previous video, happiness is a state of mind that is fleeting and never truly lasts for too very long before the opposing forces of sadness and feelings of boredom start creeping in.

Happiness is a limited resource that needs energy and time to build, and we can never really be truly happy all the time. But what about the notion of contentment?

Contentment is a state of feeling that you are satisfied with the current situation and it need not go beyond that. When we say we are contented with our circumstances, with our jobs, with our friends, family, and relationships, we are telling ourselves that we have enough, and that we can and should be grateful for the things we have instead of feeling lacking in the things we don't.

Many a times when i ask myself if i am happy about something, be it a situation that I had found myself in, or the life that I am living, majority of the time the answer is a resounding no. And it is not because I am unhappy per se, but if i were to ask myself honestly, I can't bring myself to say that yes absolutely that all is great and that I am 100$% truly happy with everything. I have to say that this is my own personal experience and it may not be an accurate representation of how you see life.

However, if i were to reframe and ask myself this question of "Am I Contented with my life?" I can with absolute confidence say yes I am. I may not have everything in the world, but i can most definitely say I am contented with my job, my friends, my family, my career, my relationships, and my health and body. That I do not need to keep chasing perfection in order to be contented with myself.

You will find that as you ask yourself more and more if you are contented, and if the answer is mostly a yes, you will gradually feel a shift towards a feeling that actually life is pretty good. And that your situation is actually very favourable. Yes you may not be happy all the time, but then again who is? As long as you are contented 90% of the time, you have already won the game of life. And when you pair contentment with a feeling of gratefulness of the things you have, you will inevitably feel a sense of happiness without having to ask yourself that question or be trying to chase it down on a daily basis.

Many a times when I looked at my current situation to see if I was on the right track, I look around me and I feel that whilst there may be areas that I am lacking and certainly needs improvement, in the grand scheme of things, I am pretty well off and i am contented.

So I challenge all of you today to look at your life in a different perspective. Start asking yourself the right question of "are you contented", and if by any chance you are not majority of the time, look at what you can do to change things up so that you do feel that life is indeed great and worth living.

I wish you guys all the success in life and I'll see you in the next one. Take care.

# Chapter 24:
# Why Are You Working So Hard

Your why,
your reason to get up in the morning,
the reason you act,
really is everything - for without it, there could be nothing.
Your why is the partner of your what,
that is what you want to achieve, your ultimate goal.
Your why will be what pushes you through the hard times on the path to your dreams.

It may be your children or a burning desire to help those less fortunate,
whatever the reason may be,
it is important to keep that in mind when faced with troubles or distractions.

Knowing what you want to do, and why you are doing it,
is of imperative importance for your life.
The tragedy is that most people are aiming for nothing.
They couldn't tell you why they are working in a certain field even if they tried.
Apart from the obvious financial payment,
They have no clue why they are there.

Is financial survival alone really a good motive to act?
Or would financial prosperity be guaranteed if you pursued greater personal preference?
Whatever your ambitions or preference in life,
make sure your why is important enough to you to guarantee your persistence.

Sometimes when pursuing a burning desire,
we can become distracted from the reason we are working.

Your why should be reflected in everything you do.
Once you convince yourself that your reason is important enough, you will not stop.
Despite the hardships, despite the fear, despite the loss and pain.
As long as you maintain a steady path of faith and resilience,
your work will soon start to pay off.
A light will protrude from the darkness and the illusionary troubles sent to test your faith will disappear as if they were never here.

Your why must be strong.
Your what must be as clear as the day is to you now.
And your faith must be eternal and unwavering.
Only then will the doors be opened to you.
This dream can be real, and will be.

When it is clear in the mind with faith, the world will move to show you the way.

The way will be revealed piece by piece, requiring you to take action and do the required work to bring your dream into reality.

Your why is so incredibly important.
The bigger your why, the greater the urgency, and the quicker your action will be.

Take the leap of faith.
Do what you didn't even know you could.
Never mind anyone else.
Taking the unknown path.
Perhaps against the advice of your family and friend,
But you know what your heart wants.

You know that even though the path will be dangerous, the reward will be tremendous.
The risks of not never finding out is too great.
The risk of never knowing if you could have done better is unfathomable.
You can always do better, and you must.

Knowing what is best for you may prove to be the most important thing for you.
How you feel about the work you are doing,
How you feel about the life you are living,
And how do you make the most of the time you have on this earth.
These may prove far more important than financial reward could ever do for you.

Aim to strike a balance.

A balance between working on what you are passionate about and building a wealthy financial life.

If your why and will are strong enough,

Success is all but guaranteed for you – no second guesses needed.

Aim for the sky,

However high you make it,

you will have proven you can indeed fly.

# Chapter 25:
# You Will Never Regret Good Work Once It is Done

Humans have debated the same things for thousands of years. More than often we get split within ourselves for whether this is right or if we are wrong. The question should never be about right or wrong. It should always be about if it suits us and others for the greater good.

Most of us spend our lives finding the answers to the questions that are born within our instincts and natural trait of curiosity. We work hard for these answers but rarely are we get satisfied with what we are doing.

We have made it so hard for ourselves to come to terms with our basic nature and level of work.

We always try to go one step ahead of others and try to prove ourselves the others. When we really should be getting more indulged in our self and our passions to get a better grip of what is going around in our lives and our loved ones.

We don't have to be proven right if we want to be content because this one approval is just the beginning.

Doing good things for the sake of just being superior is an ugly deed. But doing it for the greater good of everyone is a deed to be proud of. You should feel proud if you make someone happy but you should regret if at any time you start feeling superior for doing good.

Staying humble is the best trait a human can scrub. Even if you have all the wealth in the world.

But the thing to remember above all is that whatever you do, and whatever the outcome is, you should never feel bad or regret anything. If your intentions are pure and you put your best out there, you have no reason to feel crushed or devastated.

Life tests us in every way possible. It slaps us just when we are the most vulnerable. But the diamonds are the most difficult gems to mine. You will always find the best outcome in the harshest situations.

You only have to make sure that you don't judge your deeds based on morality, Rather you rate your efforts on a humanitarian level.

Your nature is expansive, unlike the animals with basic instincts and desires. You have to expand and explore your emotional abilities and you must try to find the deeper corners of your personality that you still haven't discovered.

Life can reward you even in the smallest of efforts. Happiness can be found in even the smallest shortest smiles that you cause.

Happiness has no definite cause, except for good intentions and the will to keep doing those things without a single grain of self profit.

But regret and shame can take root from the smallest of cracks in your will. So make sure to fill those cracks and you will turn into a skyscraper one day. Hang in there and these days will pass too.

# Chapter 26:
# The Power of Community

The topic that we are going to discuss today is something that I feel has resonated with me one a more personal level recently. And it is one that I have largely neglected in the past.

As i have mentioned before in other videos, that as an entrepreneur of sorts, my job required me to work independently, mostly from home. And while it may sound nice to others, or even yourself, where you think it is a privilege to work from home, many a times it is actually not all that fun because there is no sense of community or interaction with others. And the job becomes quite lonesome.

I'm sure many of you who have experienced lockdowns and Work from home situations, that it may seem fun for a week, but after that you realize that actually it isn't all that it is cracked out to be. And you actually do wanna get dressed, get out of the house, and go somewhere to do your work rather than stay in your PJs all day and waste your time away.

But if you dig deeper, you will realize that what you actually miss is the interaction with your co-workers, to just walk over to their desk to ask them something, or simply to just start a conversation because maybe you're bored, or to have lunch together instead of cooking your own instant noodles at home.

As social creatures, we crave that human interaction. And we crave belonging in a community and being a part of something bigger than ourselves.

When we are in lockdown, we lose that personal touch that we have with others, and we start to feel restless, we feel that something is missing but we can't put our finger on it. It is not the actual work at the job that we look forward to, but rather the people, the colleagues that make working fun and enjoyable.

The same goes for any sports of workout. You will realize that when you gym alone, you are less likely to show up because there is no one there to push you to make you do one more rep. There is no community to keep you going back to stick to your goals. For those of you who do yoga, i am sure the experience is very different when you practice an hour of yoga at home versus in a yoga studio with 30 other people, even if you don't know any of them. There is still a sense that you are a part of a greater unit, a class that works out together, a group of like-minded individuals who really want the same thing and share the same interests. You feel compelled to go back because the community is there to make the exercise fun. That after a tiring workout you look to the people beside and around you and you see the same expressions on their faces. That they had shared an activity with you and feel the same things. Isn't that what life is really about? To be a part of something rather than going about it like a lone wolf?

So for those of you who feel like something is amiss in the activity that you once loved, be it a sports or a job, or an activity that you have no choice to do but never felt happy doing it, i challenge you to find a like-minded community who share the same beliefs and interests. You can easily look for such groups on meet-up apps. You might find that the missing puzzle is indeed other individuals that share your likes. And when you work around them or with them, you will feel a much greater sense of joy and happiness that you never thought you could feel.

I hope you learned something today and I'll see you in the next one. Take care.

# Chapter 27:
# Put Yourself In Positions of Opportunity

Today I examined a story of a very famous woman in Singapore who had a less than perfect childhood, but grew up to become a big personality in the media industry. The woman I am fascinated today is the artiste known as Sharon Au.

You see, Sharon was a child of divorced parents. She moved from home to home, staying with relatives up until she was 17. Her parents were never really there for her but she had something special in her. She was resilient and she always strived to be the best.

While she did not intend to be a famous personality, she auditioned for a role as a dancer in a musical after having seen it many times before on stage, learning the songs word for word. This immediately impressed the auditioner who casted her the role of the lead.

Now we have our first example of how she had placed herself in a position of opportunity and got herself a start in what would be a lucrative career as a media personnel. The first takeaway is that she dared to try. She dared to audition. And she dared to challenge herself to be placed in a role where she could further showcase her talents. This was her at age 20.

With this first opened door, she and her cast in the musical managed to sell out 16 shows. And as luck would have it once again, she made a remarkable performance on one of the show nights while a big head of a media executive company was there to watch. She was offered a contract immediately and from there her media career took off.

She subsequently appeared in countless tv shows and became a prominent tv personality in the Singapore media industry. As her fame and popularity escalated, so did the number of opportunities in the form of contracts and endorsements that followed. She subsequently became so popular that she won numerous awards and accolades for her performance as a host and actress.

After spending more than 10 years in the media industry, she decided to pursue her initial dream of going to university at age 30. She left her lucrative entertainment career in Singapore for a university in Japan and appeared on the deans list multiple times while impressively studying and completing her education in a foreign language. She is now currently a investment director working in Paris.

I just want to impress on you today on how one decision in her life, to audition for a role in a musical, let to a chain of events that brought her much successes in her very fulfilling yet ever changing career in work and life. She had effectively placed herself in a position of opportunity one time which had led to multiple opportunities and doors opening for her like a floodgate. Barring her talent and tireless work ethic that should inspire everyone should you dig deeper into her life and career, she remains a gem in Singapore's history as an icon who had left a mark on the entertainment history even till this day.

I want to challenge all of you to not give up in placing yourself in areas where opportunities can present themselves to you. You might not know when or how it might hit you, but when it does, it can come so fast and so great that you better be prepared for it.

I hope you all enjoyed the sharing today and i hope you learned something new to improve your life and situation. As always see you in the next one.

# Chapter 28:
# *<u>Reach Peak Motivation</u>*

Remember the time when you wanted a sign, a person, a comment, an event, just anything that could maybe make you realize once again that everything is happening for real and that you actually have a presence? Remember the feeling?

I am sure we all had those times. And we often still have and maybe have some more to come. But the question is a big mystery that everyone goes through with a rough answer alongside it.

We all have a vague idea somewhere in our heads. We all have some idea somewhere wandering within us but we cease t find it with all our efforts going in vain. There is this struggle with the world that we keep fighting and then there is this quest that we always seem to be on, where we keep looking for answers.

Let me give you some tips for that. You are looking for motivation within yourself because you think the world can't do one for you. It is true to most extent, but the world is not your servant. Nature still gives you things to be proud of and be inspired from. But we keep neglecting the signs of nature.

Situations often present themselves as if we are not meant to be where we are right now. It may be true. But then the world starts to push you down, you will always find reasons at the bottom from where you would want to take a new step forward!

You will always find new ways to become motivated and inspired. Because you need to be dead to become hopeless and motionless, not wanting to do one more thing that could contribute towards a better life.

Till the day you are alive, it's a sin for you to feel hopeless and without purpose.

The fear of failure is always real. But the fear of not being able to feel content and happy once you reach the top is not a reason to not look or stop looking for newer and better things.

Life has endless possibilities and not all have to be bad always. You will get bigger and better chances more than often. But you have to remain motivated enough to avail them for better once they finally present themselves.

You don't have to be bad to fail at something. Even the best of the best fail and they fail more than a regular person. But that doesn't give them a reason to stop rather they get more motivated and energetic to stick to the cause and for what they believe in.

If one thing is important enough and you believe in it enough you will always stay connected to that thing someway or somehow.

But for that, you have to believe in your abilities. That no matter what happens, if you stay committed enough, there is no way in heaven or hell that can keep you away from success and the things that you most want in your life.

Every mountain is within reach if you keep going and keep believing that you are one more step close to the summit.

# Chapter 29:
# **NOTHING IS IMPOSSIBLE**

Success is a concept as individual as beauty is, in the eye of the beholder, but with each individuals success comes testing circumstances, the price that must be paid in advance.

The grind,

The pain and the losses all champions have endured.

These hardships are no reason to quit but an indicator that you are heading in the right direction, because we must walk through the rain to see the rainbow and we must endure loss to make space for our new desired results.

Often the bigger the desired change , the bigger the pain, and this is why so few do it.

The very fact that are listening to this right now says to me you have something extra about you.

Inside you know there is more for you and that dream you have, you believe it is possible.

If others have done it before, then so can you , because we can do anything we set our minds and hearts to.

But we must take control of our destiny, have clear results in mind and take calculated action towards those results.

The path may be foggy and unknown but as you commit to the result and believe in it the path, it will be revealed soon enough.

We don't need to know the how, to declare we are going to do something, the how will come later.

Clear commitment to the result is key.

Too many people never live their dreams because they don't know how.

The how can be found out always if we can commit and believe fully in the process.

Faith is the magic elixir to success, without it nothing is possible.

What you believe about you is everything

If you believe you cannot swim and your dream is to be an Olympic swimming champion, what are your chances?

Any rational person would say, well learn to swim,

How many of you want to be multi-millionaires?

I guess everyone?

How many out there know how to get to such a status?

Would we just give up and say it is impossible?

Or would it be as logical as simply learning how to swim or ride a bike?

We believe someone could be an Olympic swimming champion with training and practice, but not a multi-millionaire?

Many of us think big goals are simply too unrealistic.

Fear of failure, fear of what people might think, fear of change, all common reasons for aiming low in life.

But when we aim low and succeed the disappointment in that success is a foul tasting medicine.

Start gaining clarity in the reality of our results.

By thinking bigger we all have the ability to hit what seem now like unrealistic heights, but later realise that nothing is impossible.

We should all start from the assumption that we can do anything, it might take years of training but we can do it. Anything we set our minds to, we can do it.

So ask yourself right now those very important questions.

What exactly would I be doing right now that will make me the happiest person in the world? How much money do I want? What kind of relationships do I want?

When You have defined those things clearly,

Set the bar high and accept nothing less.

Because life will pay you any price.

But the time is ticking, you can't have it twice.

# Chapter 30:
# How To Stop Feeling Overwhelmed

There might come a million instances in your life when you will feel overwhelmed. Whether it's college, work, social obligations, family, or life in general, life can get anxious, stressed, and overwhelmed at certain times. It's important to recognize these feelings and give yourself grace when you have these feelings. Try to dive deeper into your emotions and understand what's causing them, don't brush them off or push through whatever's causing you to feel anxious. Your mental health matters more than anything, and if you're feeling the squeeze, know that you can always take a step back.

When things start to feel a little too much for you, take a deep breath and step away. If you feel anxious or overwhelmed, start doing some breathing exercises to alleviate those feelings. If the thing that's causing you anxiety is right in front of you, take a step away from it and create some separation between you that's overwhelming you. Deep breathing exercises will promote relaxation and would lower your stress response immediately. Understand that we all go through these phases, and it's completely okay and normal to feel like this. Cut yourself some slack and be kind towards yourself. If you're unable to do that chore or have to ask for some extension in your deadline, then do that. Your mental health should be your top priority.

While most of the time, we might want to get isolated or want everyone to leave us alone in our times of stress and anxiety, it's better to reach out to a loved one and ask for their support and help. You can also virtually chat to an online psychologist and rant to them to feel better. Or you can pick up the phone and call your friends or family and ask for their comfort and consolation.

You can also find a hobby that you find relaxation in. It can either be swimming, driving, baking, reading, or any of the stuff that calms your mind and you enjoy doing it. Writing down your reasons for anxiousness and being overwhelmed can also be a great way to alleviate those feelings. It helps you express yourself freely and provides a sense of relief once all of those thoughts are out of your head. Always remember that whatever you're feeling is temporary. With the right coping mechanisms and support, you can always take care of yourself when things start to go south. Protect your time and space and create healthy boundaries for yourself.

# Chapter 31:
# How To Rid Yourself of Distraction

Distraction and disaster sound rather similar.
It is a worldwide disorder that you are probably suffering from.
Distraction is robbing you of precious time during the day.
Distraction is robbing you of time that you should be working on your goals.
If you don't rid yourself of distraction, you are in big trouble.

It is a phenomenon that most employees are only productive 3 out of 8 hours at the office.
If you could half your distractions, you could double your productivity.
How far are you willing to go to combat distraction?
How badly do you want to achieve proper time management?

If you know you only have an hour a day to work, would it help keep you focused?

Always focus on your initial reason for doing work in the first place.
After all that reason is still there until you reach your goal.

Create a schedule for your day to keep you from getting distracted.
Distractions are everywhere.
It pops up on your phone.

It pops up from people wanting to chat at work.
It pops up in the form of personal problems.
Whatever it may be, distractions are abound.

The only cure is clear concentration.
To have clear concentration it must be something you are excited about.
To have clear knowledge that this action will lead you to something exciting.

If you find the work boring, It will be difficult for you to concentrate too long.
Sometimes it takes reassessing your life and admitting your work is boring for you to consider a change in direction.

Your goal will have more than one path.
Some paths boring, some paths dangerous, some paths redundant, and some paths magical.
You may not know better until you try.
After all the journey is everything.

If reaching your goal takes decades of work that makes you miserable, is it really worth it?
The changes to your personality may be irreversible.

Always keep the goal in mind whilst searching for an enjoyable path to attain it.

After all if you are easily distracted from your goal, then do you really want it?

Ask yourself the hard questions.
Is this something you really want? Or is this something society wants for you?

Many people who appear successful to society are secretly miserable.
Make sure you are aware of every little detail of your life.
Sit down and really decide what will make you happy at the end of your life.

What work will you be really happy to do?
What are the causes and people you would be happy to serve?
How much money you want?
What kind of relationships you want?
If you can build a clear vision of this life for you, distractions will become irrelevant.
Irrelevant because nothing will be able to distract you from your perfect vision.

Is what you are doing right now moving you towards that life?
If not stop, and start doing the things what will.
It really is that simple.

Anyone who is distracted for too long from the task in hand has no business doing that task. They should instead be doing something that makes them happy.

We can't be happy all the time otherwise we wouldn't be able to recognize it.
But distraction is a clear indicator you may not be on the right path for you.
Clearly define your path and distraction will be powerless.

# Chapter 32:
# How To Live In The Moment (Part 2)

Today we're going to talk about a different topic related to living in the moment. And this one has to do with those going through a health crisis or has a loved one who is going through one.

I hope that by the end of this video, that I will be able to encourage all of you to look at your life differently and look at how you treat your loved one who is going through a health issue with renewed eyes and perspective. Some of these concepts I derived from inspirational figures who have taught me some valuable lessons as well with their strength and resilience.

I know health can be a touchy subject. But i believe that it is something that we all struggle with at some point in our lives. When we are faced with a health scare or crisis, we will suddenly become aware of our own mortality and how fragile our lives really are. And then we start to worry about what might happen and what could happen if this and this occurs, if my health deteoriates, what that will look like, and we start scaring ourselves to no end and we start living our lives in fear that doing simple things become such a challenge for us.

I have had my fair share of health challenges. And I start worrying about the possible degradation of my body, of getting weaker, or getting old, or whatever, and get stuck in this mindset of worry. And we all know that we must not live our lives in fear, because fear is something we cannot really control. And what might happen to us is also not within our control.

What we can control however, when faced with a reality check in a health crisis, is to take stock once again of our life, the choices that we have made, health wise, eating the right foods, getting enough rest, and start fixing those things. Those are the things we can control. Another thing that is fully within our control, is to remember to live our lives in the present. When we realize time is not infinite, we need to remember to treasure each day without fear, and to start doing things now today that we won't regret. To start appreciating each day, savoring every sunset and sunrise, spending time with friends and family, and to never let ourselves get complacent with that. That we don't need multiple health scares in our lives to be reminded to live in the present and to life for the things that matter. You can't bring money with you when you die, but you can bring all your wonderful experiences at the end of your life and tell yourself that it is a life worth living. That is just me reminding u of what it might be like at the end of everyone's life, which is inevitable, this has got nothing to do with your health crisis that you are facing. I just want to be clear on that.

Another very very important thing that we need to be aware of is how we view our loved ones who are going through their own health crisis. If they have been diagnosed with something serious, and that time is of the essence, we need to show support to them by going through life with them to the fullest by spending time with them each and every day in the present moment. Live in the present with them and not worry about what could possibly happen to them. That this very second is magical with them and in this second they are alive and well. Who knows when their health could turn for the worst, and it doesn't really matter. They could live a longer life than you think. But the reality is that we never really know. And we should just cherish the present. I was inspired by this girl who suffered a terminal illness, Claire Wineland. She lived in such bravery and wisdom that she reminded everyone around her including her mom and myself, that in this moment, life is beautiful. That in this moment, life is amazing. And that in this moment, you are amazing.

So i just want to leave it as that. I hope you have been inspired today to live in the moment, in spite of fear, worries, health scares, career problems, and whatever little or big things that are weighing you down today. I hope you never forget how special this very second is.

# Chapter 33:
# Figuring Out Your Dreams

Today we're going to talk about dreams and why it is important that we all have some form of a dream or aspiration that we can work towards.

For many of us who are educated in the traditional school system, we process from one grade to the next without much thought and planning besides getting into a good school. And this autopilot has caused many kids, including myself, to not have a vision of my future and what I would like to become when I grow up. We are all taught in some shape or form that we would need to choose a career and pursue that path. Dedicating years of higher education and hundreds of hours of curriculum work only to find ourselves hating the course that we had spent all this time and energy undertaking when we step into our jobs.

This has caused many to start doubting and questioning what we ought to really do with our lives and we might get really anxious because this was certainly not part of the plan that we had set out since we were young.

What I have found personally is that I spent the time and effort to pursue a higher education not because I really wanted To, but rather to appease my parents that they did not waste all their time and money on producing me with proper schooling.

I did not however, go into my field of practice that I had spent the prior 3 years studying for. Instead upon graduating, that was when I really started to figure out what I really wanted to do with my life. Luckily for my parents, they were willing to give me the time and space to explore different possible passions and to carve out a path on my own.

I realised that as I started exploring more, and learning more about myself, the dream that I thought i once had started to change. Instead of dreaming of the perfect job and having the perfect boss, I now dreamt of freedom. To achieve freedom of time to pursue my passions, and to take steps that would move me one step closer to that dream as soon as possible.

Why this particular dream you ask? As i started exploring on successful people who have made it big in life, I realized that those that were truly happy with what they were doing, were not doing things for the money, but rather that they were able to quit their full time jobs to pursue their interests because somehow they had found a way to achieve time freedom that is irrespective of money. It amazed me how many found success by having the freedom to work from home, to not be bound by a desk job or to be hounded on my their bosses. Some live for the climb up the corporate ladder, but i knew that wasn't going to work for me. And I knew i had to make something else work to survive.

So i decided to dedicate my time and energy to only doing things that would help me achieve freedom and that became my dream to retire early and live off my past works.

The takeaway for today is that I want you to give yourself the chance to explore different things and take a step back to assess whether your current dream will actually serve you well in the long run, or if u don't even have a dream, whether you need to take time off to go find that dream for yourself.

I challenge each and everyone of you today to keep an open mind that dreams can change and you can always pursue a new path should you choose to. Because as the saying goes, the only constant in life is change.

Take care and I'll see you in the next one.

# Chapter 34:
## *Don't Be Demotivated By Fear*

What are you doing right now? What ambitions do you have for the morning to come? What doubts you have in mind? What is stopping you right now?

You have doubts about anything because you want to be cautious. You are hesitant because you have your gut telling you to think again. The reality is you are afraid and you don't know it. Or maybe you do know it but you keep ignoring your weakness.

That weakness you keep ignoring is your fear. Fear starts with a seed but if left alone can manifest deeper roots and can have a devastating impact on one's personality.

Fear is the biggest enemy of commitment. Fear kills productivity. Fear eats creativity. Fear crushes motivation.

People keep fears as if they are being smart about unexpected outcomes. You don't need to stay afraid of things to abstain from them. The only thing you need to fear is the 'Fear' itself.

When you were a child, your parents motivated you and gave you the confidence to get over most of your fears. But now you would be considered stupid and childish if you seek a mentor. You what do you do?

The answer is simple. You have yourself to try out things that make you take a step back. Because fear is self-imposed. You made yourself prone to such feelings and you can make them go away as well.

Fear can make you second guess your own abilities.

We are way behind our goals because subconsciously we have thought of the failure that can happen. The fear of our dreams shattering overtakes the ambition and happiness when you finally get to the scale. This overburdening feeling of fear keeps us sitting in our seats and stops us from trying out new things. This fear makes us believe that we don't deserve what we have dreamt of.

So I have a question for you! What have you done in the last week, or month or even a year to overcome only the smallest phobia?

If you haven't, it is possible that you won't leave what you have right now and never go for anything more than you can own. This reason is that fear makes you remain content with whatever nature and God have bestowed upon you on time after time. But you won't get up and try to work new things for bigger and better blessings that hard work and some gutsy calls have to offer.

If you can't give up the feeling of harm that might come if you finally decide to indulge in those reluctant goals, take a different approach then. Think of it as what can you be on that other side of the river? What colors does the other side of the canvas have? What laughs can you have if you made that one joke? What gains you can have if you increased just one pound?

If you try to make your fears a medium of self-analysis, maybe you start to gain the motivation that faded quickly with every second you spent in front of that source of fear. Then you might start to see a whole new image of your personality and this might be the person you always wish you could be!

# Chapter 35:
# Develop A Habit of Studying

Life is a series of lessons.
Your education does not end at 16 or 18 or 21,
It has only just begun.
You are a student of life.
You are constantly learning, whether you know it or not.

You have a free will of what you learn and which direction you go.
If you develop a habit of studying areas of personal interest,
your life will head in the direction of your interests.
If you study nothing you will be forced to learn and change through tragedy and negative circumstances.

What you concentrate on you become,
so study and concentrate on something that you want.
If you study a subject for just one hour per day, in a year you would of studied 365 hours, making you a national expert.
If you keep it up for 5 years, that's 1825 hours , making you an international expert, all from one hour per day.

If you commit to two hours you will half that time.
Studying is the yellow brick road to your dream life.
Through concentration and learning you will create that life.

Knowledge opens doors.
Being recognised as an expert increases pay.
Not studying keeps you were you are –
Closed doors and a stagnant income.

If you don't learn anything how can you expect to be valuable?
If you don't grow how can you expect to be paid more?
It only becomes too late to learn when you are dead;
until then the world is an open book will billions of pages.

Often what we deem impossible is in fact possible.
Often even your most lofty dreams you haven't even scratched the surface of what you are capable of.

Taylor your study to your goal –
follow the yellow brick road of your design.
Follow the road you have built and walk toward your goals.

If you want to be successful, study success and successful people,
then learn everything you can about your chosen field.
Plan your day with a set time for your study.
I don't care how busy you claim to be,
everybody can spare 1 hour out of 24 to work on themselves.
If not , I hope you're happy where you are,
because that is about as far as you will get without learning more.

Studying is crucial to success whether it's formal

or learning from books and online material at home.
The knowledge you learn will progress you towards your dream life.
If that is not worth an hour or two per day,
then maybe you don't want it enough and that's ok.
Maybe you want something different to what you thought,
or maybe you're happy where you are.

If not, it's on you to do this –
for yourself,
for your family,
and for your partner in life.
It's up to you to create the world you want –
A world that only you know if you deserve.

You must learn the knowledge and build the dream
because the world needs your creation.
Be a keen student of life and apply its lesson
to build your future on a solid and safe foundation.

# Chapter 36: 9 Ways To Know If You Are A Highly Sensitive Person

Being highly sensitive is personality trait that some of us may possess. Some people are born with it and some people are shaped by their life experiences, but whatever the reason is, it's there.

Barring all the articles and videos that you will find out there on this topic, my definition of a highly sensitive person is someone who has heightened emotions and sensitivity to the world around them. He or she is also a person highly driven by feelings and of the heart rather than the mind.

If you feel that you may be a highly sensitive person but aren't sure, we are going to explore today how we can identify the signs and traits of this unique personality. We will also address how you can manage your emotions when people come across too strong for your liking.

Here are 9 Ways To Know if You're A Highly Sensitive Person

1. You Pick Up On Subtile Emotional Cues

If you're a highly sensitive person, it is most likely that you're in tune with physical cues that regular people won't necessarily pick up on.

Whether it is through someone's facial expression, your inner intuition towards an unfamiliar person, or picking up hints that someone is unhappy with you even though they try to hide it very well. Being highly sensitive allows you to have a strong radar and 6th sense on these things. More often than not, you are usually right on the money.

2. Other People's Tone Is Very Important To You

If someone's tone sets you off easily, you may be a highly sensitive person without realising it. Tonality is very important to you, and you get easily put off when someone doesn't speak to you in quite the right way. Other people might have to be vary careful when communicating with you and that could be a problem in relationships if people don't understand that side of you. Communicate to others that you may be offended without meaning it, but that you will just need some time to get past it if they are unknowingly triggering you in some ways.

3. You Are Driven By Intense Emotions

Does watching a sad movie make you cry but others around you don't? Or do you feel incredibly over-the-top happy while others around you simply feel like it was just alright? If you are a highly sensitive person, it is most likely that intense emotions are what drives you. You feel the extreme end of the spectrum. You may cry your eyes out in happiness or sadness, and that's perfectly fine. Embrace your feelings and don't change anything about you.

4. You Tend To Withdraw When Things Get Too Much To Handle

When things get incredibly overwhelming, do you feel a need to just crawl away and hide instead of facing the problem head on? When we are driven my intense emotions, sometimes it can work against us. We may feel bulks of sadness and fear that paralyses us from doing anything. If that is you, considering working through these emotions one step at a time and break down the problem you face into smaller chunks.

5. You Think Deeply About Things

If you have a tendency to question about life and your existence on this earth, you may be a highly sensitive person. As you are more in tuned with the world and the mind, inevitably philosophy will be something that you will naturally gravitate towards. Entertain these thoughts and express yourself in ways that celebrate your uniqueness.

6. People And Activities Drain You

If hanging out with large groups drain you more than they energise you, or if people's problems are not something that you can handle, you may be highly sensitive. Absorbing all the energy from others can be a very exhausting experience. If you need to, take a step back and spend time alone to recharge your batteries before putting yourself out there again.

7. There's No Middle Ground

You either feel incredibly happy or incredibly sad, there's no middle ground when it comes to your emotions. You either feel happy to be around someone or you just simply want to avoid them like the plague, you don't have the patience or tolerance to perform niceties to people you feel ambivalent about.

8. You Always Feel Misunderstood

Being highly sensitive could mean that you always feel that people don't understand you or are actually hearing what you say, even if in actual fact that they are and do. You always feel a need for reassurance and double confirmation that everything is heard loud and clear. Don't fall into the trap of having to over-defend your position on something if someone doesn't seem to see eye to eye on you on certain matters. It usually isn't their fault.

9. You Love Nature More Than People

Being around other humans can be exhausting for you if you absorb and feed off their energy all the time. Sometimes nature is one that actually revitalised and recharges you. You feel at home with the birds and the trees, the tranquility, and the peace that nature brings to you. Take time out of your schedule to visit the beach, parks, and gardens energise you and release all the built up emotions that other humans and dumped on you.

# Chapter 37:
# 7 Ways To Know When It's Time To Say Goodbye To The Past

Holding on to someone or something and fearing to let go is a problem that many of us will struggle with at some point or another. Be it a partner, career, or item, a history has been built around that and we find it hard to move on and leave this treasured piece behind.

Whether it be a 6months or 10 years, it can be hard for us to come to terms with letting go because we have invested so much time, energy, and soul, into it. Governed by emotions, we hold on to them even though it may no longer bring us happiness or joy.

Whatever the reasons are, here are 7 ways that can help you say goodbye to the past and invite better things into your life:

1. You've Drag things For Way Too Long

If it's a career that you're holding on to, you may feel that you've invested a lot of effort and energy in it, waiting for the time that you will get promoted. But the days come and go, months turn into years, and you find yourself a decade later wondering what happened. Letting things drag on is no way to live life. Time is precious and every moment we waste is a moment we can never get back.

2. You Know It's Time

People may tell us we're happy and that we should be so lucky to have this job or that person in our lives, but no one can hide the unhappiness that is festering within us. Deep down in our hearts, we understand ourselves more than any other people ever would. And we know, subconsciously, if it's time to move on and let go of the past. If you are unsure, do some soul-searching. Find a time to sit by yourself quietly, or go for a retreat on your own. Sort out your feelings and bring some clarity to yourself.

3. It No Longer Brings You Joy

With a person who we have spent so much energy being a relationship with over the years, it can be hard to come to terms with the reality that he or she no longer makes you feel happy or loved anymore. Being in a constant state of unhappiness is no way to live our lives. We have every power in us to make decisions that serves us rather than hinder us. Acknowledge and accept these feelings of unhappiness. Use it as fuel to make that important decision that you know you must make.

4. You Are Holding On Out of Fear

Many a times we hold out on ending that relationship with something because we live in a constant state of fear. Career-wise we may resign ourself to the fate that things are just the way it is and we are afraid that we may never find another job again. So we hold on to that false sense of security and just drag your feet till retirement. Relationship wise, we hold on to them because we fear we may never find someone else again. So we let fear keep us in these places, feeling more and more trapped in the process.

5. You're Afraid of the Unknown

It is human nature to be afraid of the unknown. If we cannot see a clear path ahead, most of us would not dare to travel down that road. We don't know if the grass will be greener on the other side if we quit our jobs, and we don't know what the dating world will be like after being out of it for so long. We lose confidence in believing the unknown is a magical place and that wonderful things can happen there if we let ourselves take the leap of faith. That was how we got to where we were in the first place before we realized it no longer served us anymore.

6. You're Ready For Change

This is similar to the second point about knowing it's time with one key difference - you know that you ready for a new phase of life. Having the urge to intact change in your life, you believe that you don't want to be stuck in whatever situation you are in anymore. You desperately want to make things better. Embrace these feelings and start taking strong action to force change to happen for you.

7.  You Know You Deserve Happiness

Happiness has to be earned. Happiness doesn't just happen to you. If you know you deserve to be happy, and that the current thing you are holding on to only brings you sorrow, it is time to let it go. Only when you let go of what's holding you down can you make room for better and brighter things. Putting yourself out there in the face of trials and errors is the only way you can find what you are truly looking for. Demand happiness and expect it to happen to you.

Conclusion

Saying goodbye to the past is not easy, and not everyone has the courage or strength to do it. You can either choose to live in fear, or you can choose to live a brave life. It is time to make that critical decision for yourself at this crossroad right now. Only one choice can bring you the life that you truly desire. So choose wisely.

www.ingramcontent.com/pod-product-compliance
Lightning Source LLC
LaVergne TN
LVHW020446070526
838199LV00063B/4858